I0162498

MÉNAGE À TROIS

YOU, YOUR SPOUSE, & THE LOVER OF YOUR SOULS

Phil And Shae Bynes

Ménage à Trois: You, Your Spouse, and the Lover of Your Souls

ISBN 978-0692309759

Copyright © 2014 Phil and Shae Bynes. All rights reserved.

No portion of this book may be reproduced by any means - electronic, mechanical, photocopy, recording, scanning, or other - except for brief quotations in reviews or articles, without the prior written permission of the publisher. Your support of the authors' rights is appreciated.

Published by Kingdom Driven Publishing

4846 N. University Drive #406 | Lauderhill, FL 33351

Published in the United States of America

Scripture unless otherwise indicated taken from the Holy Bible, NEW INTERNATIONAL VERSION ®, NIV ® Copyright © 1973, 1978, 1984, 2011 by Biblica, Inc. ® Used by permission. All rights reserved worldwide. Scripture quotations marked (ESV) are taken from The ESV® Bible (The Holy Bible, English Standard Version®). ESV® Text Edition: 2016. Copyright © 2001 by Crossway, a publishing ministry of Good News Publishers. The ESV® text has been reproduced in cooperation with and by permission of Good News Publishers. Unauthorized reproduction of this publication is prohibited. All rights reserved. Scripture quotations marked (NKJV) are taken from the New King James Version®. Copyright © 1982 by Thomas Nelson. Used by permission. All rights reserved. Scripture quotations marked (NLT) are taken from the *Holy Bible*, New Living

Translation, copyright © 1996, 2004, 2015 by Tyndale House Foundation. Used by permission of Tyndale House Publishers, Inc., Carol Stream, Illinois 60188. All rights reserved. Scripture quotations marked (MSG) are taken from *THE MESSAGE*, copyright © 1993, 2002, 2018 by Eugene H. Peterson. Used by permission of NavPress. All rights reserved. Represented by Tyndale House Publishers, Inc.

Acknowledgment

It has been ten years since the initial release of this book in 2014. We considered writing an updated version to celebrate the 10th anniversary for the book (and our 25th wedding anniversary), but ultimately did not feel led to add anything new. We pray that you are blessed by these lessons Holy Spirit taught us ten years ago that still guide us today!

Love, Phil and Shae

Contents

Introduction

We never planned to write a book like the one you're about read. We've always enjoyed sex during our marriage, but we didn't spend much time speaking to others about it and certainly never discussed writing a book about it! We haven't experienced any significant challenges in the bedroom during our 15 years of marriage, however when the Lord showed up in our bedroom we realized that there was so much more to experience that we had been missing out on.

This book shares eight lessons given to us by the Holy Spirit (during the middle of sex or immediately following) over a period of several months. We understand that this is peculiar, but apparently the Teacher of all Teachers felt that "on the job training" would be most effective. It was all rather strange in the beginning, but then we embraced it and starting keeping a notebook and tablet on each of our nightstands in preparation for our next lesson. Sometimes those lessons would come within days, but most often within weeks. We are not sex therapists nor licensed marriage counselors. We are simply a loving couple with an awesome assignment from the Lord to impact married couples (both inside and outside of the bedroom) through the power and love of God.

From our bedroom and hearts to yours, we pray that these lessons will transform your relationship and further establish Christ's position at the center of your marriage. May God be glorified and may Heaven be released in your bedroom.

P.S. If you're single, be inspired but proceed cautiously. This book was truly written for those who are married or have a wedding date set on the calendar. Married couples, we encourage you to read, discuss, and put to practice what is shared. We've provided questions and scriptures to help facilitate meaningful discussion to go along with that practice! Engaged couples, let's save some of that "putting to practice" for later, shall we? Enjoy the adventure!

Bedroom Lesson #1

The Lord Wants to Be Involved in Your Bedroom

It's important to set a proper foundation right away because without it many of the other bedroom lessons will be hard to receive and embrace. As a Christian couple you should experience more of the fullness of God and the love of Jesus Christ in your marriage, and what happens in your bedroom plays a significant role. Let's begin by addressing a couple of common myths among Christian couples (and please don't skip a section thinking "I don't believe in that myth!" because you just might miss something important).

Myth #1: *"The Lord doesn't care about our sex life."*

False. God cares about *every detail* that concerns you and your marriage. As your Creator and the Maker of your covenant relationship as husband and wife, He desires to be involved in every area of your marriage....and that includes between the sheets. If you think about it, if the scripture instructs us not to have sex before marriage, it means that He is concerned about sex. God is intentional. He isn't going to stop caring about your physical intimacy now that you're within the covenant of marriage. It's about intimacy and love. Can you truly "make love" without God when He IS love? When you make Jesus Christ the center of your marriage, know that everything can be yielded to Him. Nothing should be off limits to place at His feet and in His hands.

Far too often we compartmentalize our lives and only give the Lord access to certain aspects of it. We operate our daily lives without awareness of, or regard for, God's presence and His guidance. He didn't leave you alone to figure out how to do this marriage thing all by yourselves. There's no way you could do this on our own and do it well! He has made power, wisdom, and the ability to both receive and give love unconditionally available to you. Not only that, but He stays with you. Yes, the very presence of God is with you and your spouse at all times and you have the Holy Spirit within you, guiding you, teaching you, comforting you, and leading you from moment to moment in your marriage.....if you allow Him to do so.

The Holy Spirit will help you to avoid turning what's supposed to be a wonderful thing like sex into an argument. Wives, have you ever experienced boredom in the bedroom because your husband has become predictable? You think to yourself "I showed excitement about that ONE time and now he thinks he should do it all the time!" Well, instead of having an argument or holding a grudge, isn't it great to know that the Holy Spirit is willing and able to give insight to your husband? Husbands, have you ever needed a little help with your wife getting her interested in being the initiator of sex more often? Jesus is the best wingman you could ever have (more on that later)!

Why does the Lord care about being involved in every aspect of your marriage, both inside and outside of your bedroom? Because He loves you without measure. Everything God has ever done, everything He is currently doing, and all that He has yet to do is motivated by His amazing love for you. Absolutely nothing can separate you from the love of your Savior Jesus Christ. He died for you, was raised to life, and is now sitting at the right hand of the Father, pleading on your behalf. Because of that love, you can (and should) trust and lean on Him when it comes to your bedroom activities.

Myth #2: *"It's really not right to think about Jesus when we're having sex."*

Wrong. This is an unfortunate, destructive, and limiting mindset that has led many couples astray and into divorce court. Sex is a spiritual matter, greater than simply a procreation or even recreational matter. Your awesome Creator....well, He created it. He ought to be acknowledged, praised, and glorified through your physical intimacy. That physical expression of love should be offered as worship to the Lord. There is an overflow created in your bedroom that will extend outside of your bedroom and have an impact in every area of your marriage and family life.

SHAE: A Bedroom Invasion

I remember the first time the Lord made His way into our bedroom a couple years ago. My husband Phil and I had just finished making love and I was laying on his chest. I certainly wasn't thinking about Jesus; it was more of a "basking in the afterglow" and "Wow, I really love this dude" kind of moment. Imagine my surprise when I heard the following words: "You know how loved you feel right at this moment? I love you way more than that!"

I didn't hear these words audibly, but yet I heard them so clearly in my spirit. My eyes filled with tears and I laid there and cried because I knew without a doubt that was the Lord speaking to me. It wasn't just the words He said, but the way He said it. It was so full of love and

and He emphasized the word "way" so it sounded more like "waaaaaaaaaaaaaaaaaay more than that!" I had to explain to Phil why I was crying. I think he made a joke about how Jesus "one-upped" him, but it was a special and revelatory moment. It was not only a wonderful reminder of how loved I was, but the fact that the Lover of My Soul chose that very moment to speak to me revealed something important that neither of us had considered in over a decade of marriage – the tangible presence of God resides in our bedroom and He doesn't disappear simply because we're having sex. He's present and desires to commune at a time when we typically wouldn't even be thinking of Him.

This was the beginning of the fun journey of bedroom discovery that lied ahead of us; a journey that turned those passionate heat of the moment cries of "Oh my God" (you know what I'm talking about!) to a heartfelt reverence and worship of "Oh....my God!"

Having a ménage à trois with the Lover of your Souls within the covenant of marriage is handling Kingdom Business! The Kingdom of God is God's system; His way of being and doing things. When you align with Him in the bedroom, the results will be far-reaching and you will experience more than you can ask for or even think to ask for within your marriage.

How To Invite the Lord in Your Bedroom

You (or perhaps your spouse) may not yet be convinced that you actually want to invite the Lord in your bedroom. If you're not, that's ok and we believe you'll have a change of heart before finishing this book. If you are ready to invite Him in, you may be wondering how exactly to do that. Here are a couple of ways:

Recognize God and praise Him - This is a conscious effort and a matter of your heart. Psalm 100:4 encourages us to enter His gates with thanksgiving in our hearts and to enter His courts with praise. Make having a grateful heart part of your foreplay. Husbands, you can simply say (in your mind, doesn't even have to be out loud) "Thank you Lord for giving me such an awesome and beautiful wife. I didn't even have to twist her arm to make her love me. You even made sure she has all the curves I wanted...and she takes such good care of me." Wives, you may be saying "Lord, I thank you for this awesome man of God you've placed in my life. I love how he sings to me and so grateful that he washed those dishes earlier today...and he's FINE too? Lord, you have just outdone yourself!" We're not giving you scripts here. The idea is to give thought to and give thanks to God for those things you appreciate about your spouse. As you praise, you've just entered the gates of the Kingdom of God.

Simply say a prayer together - Share your heart with each other and with the Lord through prayer right now. Invite the Lord to have His way in you and in your bedroom. Let Him know that you want to know more of His goodness and see more of His glory in your marriage. Let Him know that you desire more of His presence.

Questions To Ask Each Other & Discuss:

1. How do you feel about inviting Jesus in our bedroom?

2. What does worship mean to you? Can you see how sex can be offered as worship?

3. What are 3 things that you appreciate most about me?

Bedroom Lesson #2

Intimacy with Each Other Begins with
Intimacy with God

Do you remember the dating and courting process with your spouse before you were married? You spent time getting to know each other, sharing about yourself, sharing your goals, and developing a friendship. You experienced enough during those pre-marital months or years to know that this is the person you desire to commit to and spend the rest of your life with. The day you went before God and committed yourselves to each other in marriage marked just the beginning of what was to come. Can you imagine if you stopped interacting after the wedding and said to yourself "Ok I'm married now. This is what I've been waiting for and now I'm satisfied"? That's not what we do and it even sounds silly. You desire so much more – fellowship, friendship, family.

This is unfortunately what happens to many believers who give their lives to Jesus Christ. They receive the "ultimate prize of salvation" and are satisfied. Like your wedding day is just the beginning for you and your spouse, salvation is just the beginning for your relationship with God. Eternal and abundant life begins when you accept Christ as your personal savior. We were created for relationship with our Creator! His desire is to have a deep, personal, and intimate relationship with you and to be not only Savior, but Lord. God called Abraham His friend. Jesus said to the disciples in John 15:15 "I no longer call you servants, because a servant does not know his master's business. Instead, I have called you friends, for everything that I learned from my Father I have made known to you." In friendship there is intimacy; closeness, trust, and sharing.

Notice that intimacy doesn't mean sex. It is closeness, trust, sharing, fellowship, and friendship. You can have intimacy without sex and you can have sex when there's no intimacy, even within marriage. What happens if you're suddenly unable to have sex due to medical conditions or other physical reasons? Intimacy with each other will stand and hold your relationship together. It is essential for a healthy and thriving marriage. To live submitted to one another as husband and wife as the scripture instructs (Ephesians 5:21), and to enjoy really amazing sex, the intimacy you need begins with your intimacy with God. Here's why:

Intimacy with God enables you to receive His love, learn His love, and give His love.

Romans 5:5 tells us that the love of God has been poured into our hearts by the Holy Spirit which means that you have the ability to love others unconditionally as He loves you. You can't fully understand the immeasurable love that God has for you, but Christ will make His home in your heart as you place your trust in Him, rooting and grounding you in the love of God. Receiving His love comes through your heart, not through intellectual understanding of the scriptures. He chose you and He cares about every single detail of your life and it is through intimate fellowship with Him that you will experience that truth in practical ways in your everyday life.

Ephesians 5:1-2 (The Message) says "Watch what God does, and then you do it, like children who learn proper behavior from their parents. Mostly what God does is love you. Keep company with him and learn a life of love. Observe how Christ loved us. His love was not cautious but extravagant. He didn't love in order to get something from us but to give everything of himself to us. Love like that." There's a lot of goodness in that verse, but note that is says "keep company with him," and that is fellowship. That is intimacy.

The result of keeping company with Him is that you learn a life of love that is extravagant for not only our spouses, but for everyone. God's love is perfected (developed and matured) in us through a dynamic relationship where we both dwell in His love (through union and fellowship with Him) and express that love to one another. We increase our capacity to receive God's love in order to give it away, and yet we need to give it away in order to increase our capacity to receive!

Intimacy with God gives you the ability to hear and recognize His voice.

A lifestyle of intimacy with God strengthens your spirit and makes it more sensitive to the things of the Spirit. This is key to hearing His voice more clearly and discerning between the voice of the Lord and the voices that come from your own mind, will, or even the enemy. You're going to need to hear and recognize the voice of the Lord to be effective as a husband or wife. God knows your spouse better than you do. He knows YOU better than you know yourself.

Intimacy with God purges you from religious and legalistic mindsets.

A spirit of religion will extinguish the fire in your marriage with a quickness because it hinders relationship. A religious spirit turns God into a taskmaster rather than the loving Father He is. It focuses on performance-based relationship, denominational rules and regulations. It's judgmental, prideful, joyless, close-minded, stagnant...it's anti-Christ. When you enjoy intimacy with the Lord, your fire is ignited, your heart burns for Him and for others, and your light shines in your relationships. Your heart and spirit remain open to how the Holy Spirit moves and guides you in every area of your marriage, inside and outside of the bedroom.

Experiencing True Intimacy with God

How do you begin to experience true intimacy with God? An entire book can be written on this topic, but there are a few things we recommend. First, recognize that intimacy with God includes a closeness and fellowship with every part of Him -- Father, Son, and Holy Spirit. It is through Christ we have both access to the Father by one Spirit (Ephesians 2:18). Intimacy is cultivated by time, communication, and trust.

Time: Make spending private time with the Lord on a regular basis a priority. Relationships require time. Break away from the busyness to spend time in His presence with a heart to know Him more. There are no rules about where to spend the time and how much time to spend. Your time may be in a long shower, in the car during a long commute to work, in your favorite cozy spot in your home. You may spend 15 minutes, 30 minutes, 2 hours. The key is spending time that is completely devoted to Him.

Communication: Communicating with the Lord includes both talking *and* listening. So often we have a limited view of what prayer is; we think that prayer is simply talking to God. When the scripture says "pray without ceasing" it doesn't mean bow your head and close your eyes all day. It's an ongoing fellowship and communication with an attitude of awareness and surrender. The Holy Spirit will fellowship with you all day long! He will talk to you about the average ordinary everyday things that you're doing. He is actively involved in the little things as well as the big things. He helps us in our marriage all the time! He helps us avoid unnecessary arguments by directing us when to shut our mouths and when to open them. He helps us know as soon as our spouse walks in the door what kind of day they had and how we can best serve them. He will even guide you during your sexual intimacy with "Don't do that. Do this." He cares about every single detail. That is His abundant love in action!

Spend time just sitting at the feet of Jesus. Meditate on the scripture by asking the Holy Spirit to show you what He would have you to read and meditate on. Ask Him to give you wisdom, understanding and revelation of His Word. Ask Him to show you His heart. Journal what He shares with you. Even journaling is a time of fellowship.

Trust: Demonstrate your faith and trust in God by being obedient to His Word concerning you. Obedience is the evidence that you are living in God. As you're communicating with the Lord and receive instructions from Holy Spirit, trust and obey. Lean on Him, depend on Him, interact with Him, and allow Him to lead and guide you. When you keep Him in His proper position and surrender to His will, you will be a true son or daughter of God and experience the greater things He has in store for you.

While intimacy isn't about sex, sex between a husband and wife is a beautiful expression of intimacy that truly gives you a slice of Heaven on earth. Jesus lives within you and wants to express Himself through you in every area of your marriage. Intimacy with God is the foundation of being a reflection of Him to your spouse.

Questions To Ask Each Other & Discuss:

1. Do you feel like you have an intimate relationship with God?

2. How do you talk to God and how does He speak to you?

3. Have you ever experienced Holy Spirit giving you an instruction that helped you in our marriage? Tell me about it.

Bedroom Lesson #3

Your Bedroom Is a Well

The Merriam-Webster dictionary defines a well as *a deep hole made in the ground through which water can be removed.* Another definition is *a source from which something may be drawn as needed.* Your bedroom is a powerful place to dig a well; a place where you pour in the anointing of God, create a pool, and draw living water from. In John 7, the Bible tells the story of Jesus at the Festival of Tabernacles, where after teaching in the temple courts He stood and cried out "If anyone thirsts, let him come to Me and drink. He who believes in Me, as the Scripture has said, out of his heart will flow rivers of living water." Jesus was referring to believers being filled by the Holy Spirit so they would not only be satisfied in Him, but also experience an overflow that will serve as a blessing to those around them.

SHAE: Digging Our Own Well

Once we started digging a well in our own bedroom, we found over time that God meets us more in our bedroom than any other place in our house. His presence shows up more often and at a greater level. It's almost like the Lord is saying "I'm welcome here!" and so He meets us in the place where we welcome Him. It has become our meeting spot. We're more inspired there. We have God-filled dreams there. We hear the voice of the Lord with more clarity there. We experience visions there. We express our love to each other in even greater ways there.

The living water we draw from the well we've dug not only benefits us as a couple, but our entire family as well. The overflow begins in your home and extends outside of your home to others, even to difficult people.

The truth is that any place can be a well. Your car can be a well. The shower can be a well. Your closet, your kitchen, your home office....any of these places can be a well. He wants to be where you are. He wants to be where you're acknowledging Him. Want to experience Heaven in your bedroom, including between the sheets? Dig a well and create an atmosphere in your bedroom where the Lord is welcomed. When He is your dwelling place, He makes His home with you. Psalm 91:9-10 says:

"Because you have made the Lord, who is my refuge,

Even the Most High, your dwelling place,

No evil shall befall you,

Nor shall any plague come near your dwelling."

Make Him your dwelling place, and He shows up in ways that you may not have ever expected or imagined.

PHIL: Jesus is My Wingman

You may be familiar with the concept of a wingman. When a guy needs a little help making progress with a woman of interest, he may ask another guy to serve as his wingman and help him out. You've probably seen a wingman in action on television or in the movies; it's typically in a dating or frivolous one night stand scenario. You'd think that as a married man I wouldn't need a wingman, but you'd be wrong. Sometimes I need a little help with my wife and I suspect husbands reading this may need a little help too at times. I discovered that when I invited Jesus into our bedroom and dug a well, He became my wingman. Allow me to share a quick story with you.

One evening I went upstairs to my bedroom and my wife was sound asleep. I was looking at her and thinking it would be really nice to have some fun, but I knew waking her up would be a terrible idea because she was out cold. The kind of sleep that if I woke her up, I would've received something other than what I was looking for! I was laying on her back, just thinking about my desire to make love to her and she popped up out of her sleep and said "What are you doing to me?" I replied "Nothing, I'm not doing anything." She woke up out of a deep sleep ready to go and we had a wonderful time. Jesus was my wingman! All I had to do was have a thought and He came through for me.

You may be laughing, but this just another example of how He cares about all of the details and the desires of my heart. The battle was not mine. It was the Lord's. It was as if Jesus said "I know some people. I can hook you up. I will decree it and it will be established for you...just because you're my boy." That's the King of kings making things happen. He's a heavyweight loving champ. He knows how to serve better than any of us. He can be your wingman too! I'm not saying that digging a well in your bedroom is only about having Jesus as your wingman. He is so much bigger than that and that is just one of countless ways that inviting Him in has served my marriage.

How To Dig A Well

By now you may be wondering how you dig a well in your bedroom (or anywhere else for that matter). The heart of it is creating an atmosphere where God is welcomed. The more time you spend pursuing God, thinking about the things of God, talking about the things of God together, the broader and deeper the well becomes. Spend time praying together while in your bedroom (not necessarily before or after sex… just in general) as a consistent way of seeking the Lord together and cultivating a lifestyle of intimacy with Him. Jesus said that when two or more are gathered in His name, He is in the midst, so by spending that time in prayer in your bedroom, you have already welcomed Him in.

Another key to digging a well in your bedroom is offering up your sexual intimacy as worship to the Lord. We discussed this briefly in Lesson #1. God ought to be acknowledged, praised, and glorified through your physical intimacy. You may be thinking "Worship? During sex?" Yes! Worship is a humble attitude and reverence toward God for who He is. It's an acknowledgement of His power, goodness, and love. It is an intimacy that produces the abundant life (to the full, till it overflows) that Christ laid down His own life for on your behalf. Worshipping between the sheets isn't as strange as it may sound. It's simply a decision you make in your heart that says "Lord, it's my desire to please you through this time of intimacy with my husband/wife" and an invitation to the Holy Spirit to lead and guide you in your bedroom affairs.

God is larger than you think, more majestic than you can imagine and takes more pleasure in your worship than you know. Worship leads to a manifestation of God's presence. Worship establishes Heaven on earth. The simple truth is you cannot out give God. If you give Him your bedroom, He will give you Himself in your bedroom and that is a beautiful thing.

Questions To Ask Each Other & Discuss:

1. Have you personally dug a well anywhere inside or outside of our home? Tell me about an experience or encounter you had with the Lord there.

2. What would Heaven on earth in our marriage look like to you?

Bedroom Lesson #4

Sow into the Spirit, Not the Flesh

When we think of books we've read and even the rare sermons we've heard on the topic of physical intimacy within marriage, much of the advice has centered around the fact that there is freedom in the bedroom and it's ok to be "freaky" (because after all, the marriage bed is undefiled). This advice is understandable because there are so many Christian couples that struggle in areas of sexual expression with each other due to feelings of guilt, shame, and embarrassment. We've also found that often the wives are encouraged to ensure they are having sex often and keeping their husbands sexually satisfied so they are not tempted. There are elements of truth to all of this, but it's incomplete and unbalanced; without wisdom from the Holy Spirit, it can be downright disastrous. We will address the unbalance first so we can get to the "good" and then share some insight that will reveal the "great" for what takes place between your sheets.

The Undefiled Marriage Bed

Undefiled means *pure, having no faults, sinless.* A popular (incompletely) quoted scripture is Hebrews 13:4 "The marriage bed is undefiled" which at quick glance seems to indicate that no fault can be found in your sexual activities as long as you're married. Let's take a look at what Hebrews 13:4 actually says: Marriage *is* honorable among all, and the bed undefiled; but fornicators and adulterers God will judge (NKJV). Other translations bring even more clarity:

Marriage should be honored by all, and the marriage bed kept pure, for God will judge the adulterer and all the sexually immoral. (New International Version)

Honor marriage, and guard the sacredness of sexual intimacy between wife and husband. God draws a firm line against casual and illicit sex. (The Message)

Let marriage be held in honor (esteemed worthy, precious, of great price, and especially dear) in all things. And thus let the marriage bed be undefiled (kept undishonored); for God will judge and punish the unchaste [all guilty of sexual vice] and adulterous. (Amplified)

What comes to mind as you read these other translations? Doesn't it sound less like a license to be as freaky as you want to be and more like an admonishment to be honorable to your spouse (and therefore honorable to God) in your sexual intimacy? Don't get us wrong. There IS freedom in your marriage bed. Where the Holy Spirit is, there is liberty and the Holy Spirit dwells on the inside of you. You're not in bondage or oppression; you have the freedom of the Holy Spirit working in your lives (2 Corinthians 3:17). The Lord's desire is that we take that freedom granted to us, and we yield our wills up to Him and follow His will concerning us.

Honoring Your Spouse in the Bed

There is certainly freedom in your marriage bed, but does that mean anything goes? No, the Bible tells us that we need to hold our sexual intimacy as sacred and honorable. What does it mean to honor your husband or wife in the bed? It means to esteem and hold your spouse in high regard. It means to care and be sensitive about the needs of your spouse. You may think you can do this on your own, but the truth is that you need the Holy Spirit's involvement. You need to know His voice. Why? Because the Lord is aware of deep issues that you're not aware of, and quite frankly your spouse may not be aware of them either.

The Bible doesn't speak directly on most specifics of sexual intimacy between a husband and wife. There are no hard and fast rules despite what you may have heard from religious leaders. Certainly the involvement of another man or woman would be adultery, but more common things such as oral sex, sex with toys, creative positions, digital penetration, hand jobs – all of these are lawful, but not all of them are beneficial. The Holy Spirit desires a relationship with you so that He can instruct you about what to do and what not to do in your own marriage bed. It's not about what your pastors are doing in their bed. It's not about what your friends are doing in their bed. It's not about what your therapist is doing in his or her bed. This is a private matter – one that is not just between you and your spouse, but between you, your spouse, and the Lover of your Souls.

Here are some real scenarios that may help you understand how important this is. A husband could've struggled in years past with pornography, and while he has only watched it once or twice in the five years that you've been married, there are certain things you may do in your bed that serve as triggers and open a door for the enemy. A wife may have been molested as a young child or pre-teen and there are certain things the husband may want (and expect) sexually that make the wife feel uncomfortable. Sometimes it's not something as horrific as a molestation or a rape. Perhaps it's not a stronghold such as pornography. However there are a variety of issues, mindsets, past experiences that husbands and wives deal with that can impact intimacy and if left to your own devices without the Holy Spirit, you can create more problems. On the other hand, with the Lord invited into your intimate affairs, healing from these issues can take place right in the midst of intercourse. We can assure you that this is *not* the kind of sexual healing that Marvin Gaye sang about, but the amazing healing power of God. When you sow into the spirit versus the flesh, this is an example of the "great" that you can experience.

Sowing Into the Flesh vs. Sowing Into Spirit

You're probably familiar with the Biblical principle of sowing and reaping (the law of the harvest). It's not simply an agricultural principle, but also a life principle which states that whatever you sow, you're also going to reap. Galatians 6:7 says a man reaps what he sows. The Amplified version says "For whatever a man sows, that and that only is what he will reap." This is commonly understood to mean that whatever seeds we're planting (positive or negative), will return to us and we'll receive more than we actually planted.

How does this principle apply to sexual intimacy and experiencing God's best? When we're having sex, we make a choice (intentionally or unintentionally) to sow to the flesh or sow to the spirit.

PHIL: "I'm Not In That!"

While making love to my wife one morning, we both felt the presence of God enter the room. We had crossed over to a point of worship and honoring Him and acknowledging His presence. I was the first to climax, so during my recovery time I decided to satisfy my wife by "letting my fingers do the walking" and immediately after she had an orgasm I heard the Spirit of the Lord say "I'm not in that!" I said to Him (in my spirit, not audibly) "Excuse me Lord, repeat that phrase to me again" and I heard it again very clearly, "I'm not in that!" and I could tell that His presence wasn't as close.

The best way I can explain it is that it was as if He was casually leaning against the wall with His arms crossed waiting. He directed me to place my hand on my wife's belly and instantly she began to respond to the presence of God in a manner that was a marked difference from what she experienced just moments prior to that. It was as if I had tagged Him back into the game!

The Lord revealed to me that there is a difference between the response of flesh to the...and the flesh to the spirit. If we want the greater, there is an order to things. He showed me that when we are completely aligned with His natural design and purpose that He will come in and overlay Himself on us, but when we operate outside of the order He desires, He has to watch from the sidelines waiting for an opportunity to participate.

I asked the Lord if I had sinned because of the digital penetration. The response I received was not necessarily, but it was sowing into the flesh and He had no place in that. The issue wasn't in the action; the issue was in the focus. Our intent and original focus was worship to God, but then it shifted to a focus on an orgasm. I was thinking to myself "I didn't bring her to completion and I can't really get it up right now. I know what I'll do!" so I took matters into my own hands to avoid ruining my track record and in doing so, I removed God from first place.

Making climax an idol is one of the main signs that you're sowing to the flesh in your sexual intimacy. It seems like a selfless act, ensuring that your husband or wife experiences that highly anticipated orgasm – the pinnacle of sexual intimacy. Other ways you can make climax an idol is *insisting* that the intercourse continues until you get yours or until they get theirs multiple times, and defaulting to masturbation to finish the job that was deemed incomplete. You don't have to be self-sufficient in your sexual relationship. Even if you are experiencing challenges in your sexual intimacy, yield those challenges to the Lord. Your Heavenly Father is the Source of healing and the Source of unlimited wisdom. Through His Son Jesus Christ and in His Spirit, you can access everything needed to get things right.

Sowing Into the Spirit

John 3:6-7 says "That which is born of flesh is flesh, and that which is born of the Spirit is spirit. Do not marvel that I said to you that you must be born again." When you sow into the spirit, you will receive from the Spirit which means that you've created a welcomed place for God to join Himself to what you're doing. When you sow into the spirit, you yield the fruit of the Spirit – love, joy, peace, patience (longsuffering), kindness, goodness, faithfulness, gentleness, and self-control (Galatians 5:22-25). Not only do you reap the fruit of the Spirit (which will extend well beyond the four corners of your bed), but you will also create an atmosphere for the Lord to have His way and do whatever is needed to release Heaven in your relationship. Reaping from the Spirit always trumps reaping from the flesh.

So how do you sow into the spirit? It's actually quite simple and it starts with your "seeker." When you seek first the Kingdom of God and His righteousness, everything else you need will be added to you (Matthew 6:33). Seeking the Kingdom of God means going in quest of God's way of being and doing things. God looks at your heart. Once you've decided in your heart that you desire to worship God and honor your husband or wife through sex, you can ask the Holy Spirit "How do you feel about this? Is this pleasing to you?" during those moments of physical intimacy. You won't find yourself asking the question all of the time because over time your intimacy with the Holy Spirit will make it an unnecessary question to ask (you'll know the answers in your heart).

If you're having challenges with pleasing each other in the bedroom, remember that the Holy Spirit is your Helper. He's your Comforter, Helper, Teacher, and so much more. You have to learn to hear His voice and that comes with your own intimate time in fellowship with Him. The Holy Spirit also convicts, so if you're feeling convicted about anything that you're doing in the bedroom, seek His guidance while being sensitive and honest with your spouse about the conviction you're feeling. You can trust that God will work on the heart of your spouse.

SHAE: Guess What? It's Fun!

I can hear some of you thinking "Dang Phil and Shae, you're taking all the fun out of sex! This is just too deep!" but I can assure you that a ménage à trois with the Lover of your Souls is anything but boring. Sure we have our favorite positions and activities, but there's plenty of variety and plenty of surprises. Our imagination is supposed to be a hot bed for God, but often times the enemy perverts it. When you give God back control over your imagination, the results are pure and exciting thanks to His creative ability working through you. I could even tell you stories about three different occasions when I experienced orgasms without even being touched, but that's not the objective of this book.

There's another perk we've discovered about sowing into the spirit instead of the flesh. Maybe it's just us, but when Phil was sowing into the flesh, he experienced a physical emptiness after an orgasm which led to a hard crash of energy. He'd be asleep within moments. I would feel a void after an orgasm that could only be filled by cuddling up afterwards...and that void couldn't be filled when Phil was asleep. Now that we focus on sowing into the spirit, we always feel full and typically eager for the next worship experience! We can both transition into a peaceful sleep or first enjoy some non-physical moments together, but the void is no longer there.

Here's something amazing about the Lord that you should know if you don't know it already -- whatever you have a hunger for when it comes to the things of God, He will satisfy it! Are you looking to "spice things up"? Moving beyond the shallow waters to experience the deeper things of God in the bedroom is an awesome way of doing just that. You can have the good...it's permissible, but why not enjoy the great!

Questions To Ask Each Other & Discuss:

1. How can I best honor you in our sexual intimacy?

2. Is there anything that we do in the bedroom that makes you uncomfortable?

3. Are we making a climax an idol? How so? What can we do to change that? Do you want to change that?

4. Have you ever felt convicted by the Holy Spirit regarding something we've done in the bedroom?

5. What does "sowing into the spirit" look like to you? How can we begin to do that more in our physical intimacy?

Bedroom Lesson #5

What's Your Soundtrack?

Music is powerful. Without delving into the details of decades of modern scientific research on the psychological and physiological effects of music, we can likely agree on two key points:

Music impacts our emotions: Music can evoke profound emotions. The emotions vary based on the individual and the type of music, but we're sure that you can think back to times (probably not too long ago) where music brought forth feelings of happiness, sadness, gratitude, peacefulness, or even anger or aggravation.

Music is intimately linked to our memory: Music triggers vivid memories that take us back to personal experiences, emotional responses, specific objects, people, places, and events from our past. Numerous studies have shown that we don't even have to hear the music because simply the lyrics are enough to elicit memories.

The power of music isn't referenced solely in scientific studies, it is also referenced in the scriptures. After all, music began in the heart of God and has a purpose in His design. When King Saul was troubled by distressing spirits, young David would play a harp. Saul would be "refreshed and well, and the distressing spirit would depart from him." (1 Samuel 16) When Elisha was asked to share the word of the Lord to King Jehoshaphat and the kings of Israel and Edom, he summoned a musician to enable him to prophesy (2 Kings 3:14-15). There are a number of examples in the Word where God responded to music that was used to glorify Him.

If you're committed to offering up your sexual intimacy as worship unto the Lord, you can't ignore the impacts of music in your intimacy. The questions that you and your spouse should ask yourselves are: What's our soundtrack? What music and lyrics are being released into our atmosphere? What is speaking to our hearts and our spirits as we express our love to each other?

The Power of Your Bedroom Soundtrack

Music takes you to another place in time and the implications of this can be both beneficial and detrimental to your marriage. One of the downfalls is that music can elicit unhealthy memory triggers due to soul ties. A soul tie is an emotional bond that unites you with someone else – it's a binding through your soul (mind, will, and emotions). There are both healthy and unhealthy soul ties that are created through close friendships, physical intimacy, commitments and vows. Imagine for a moment the implications of these memory triggers during times of physical intimacy with your spouse:

- That song you played during sex with other men or women you previously dated (or just had a little rumble in the sack with)

- Those songs you played during sex with your ex-husband or ex-wife

- Those songs that played at the wedding and/or reception when you married your ex-husband / ex-wife

You can probably also imagine other unhealthy memory triggers that could happen such as the song you were listening to while you were dancing at the nightclub with that gorgeous man or woman in your pre-marriage days, or the song that was playing on that crazy night at your friend's bachelor party when you got a lap dance (and enjoyed it). Do you really want to be thinking about these other people while you're enjoying a time of intimacy with the love of your life? One way to combat that is by changing your soundtrack.

You may not have any of these experiences. That's great news, but you're not out of the woods yet. There are other implications to your soundtrack choice that we need to discuss, and we'll start with a confession. We did not wait until we were married to have sex (Mom & Dad, we're sorry to break the news to you this way). We have been together since we were juniors in high school, and while we made it through high school, the summer after graduation we gave in to the pressure and the desire to experience each other in a new and exciting way.

Over the next five years of dating, music played a significant role in making it very difficult to avoid doing the things we knew in our hearts that we had no business doing as believers in Christ. We loved the Lord and often said we'd stop having sex, but there was a gate that we did a horrible job of protecting – the "ear gate." Colossians 3:2 urges us to set our mind on things above, not worldly things, but with no protection of the ear gate we continuously allowed the Top 20 R&B hits to flood our souls and remind us of those wonderful feelings we'd be missing out on if we stopped having sex (somehow we weren't reminded about the guilt often felt afterwards). During our college years we lived in separate cities four hours apart, so you can imagine the anticipation that was built up during the car rides on the way to see each other every couple of months, listening to our favorite love songs.

We share this to illustrate what you probably have experienced as well, and that is the emotional response created by music and particularly by lyrics. Yes, there is freedom in your marriage bed, but what thoughts do you want to have going on in your mind while you're enjoying each other? Much (but not all) of the lyrics in popular "love songs" across genres are about lust (at best) and adultery (at worst) – sowing into the flesh and not to the spirit.

Shifting the Atmosphere

If you desire to create an atmosphere that is conducive for expressing a pure love for each other, avoiding unhealthy memory triggers, and welcoming the entrance of the Holy Spirit, give an attentive ear to your soundtrack and make changes as needed. The music doesn't have to be labeled traditionally as worship music, although it certainly can be. You may want to consider love songs by Christian music artists, anointed instrumental music, or no music at all (nothing wrong with making your own).

The truth is that many Christian husbands and wives don't spend much time thinking about the music they listen to in general, much less in the bedroom during sex. Music choice is a touchy subject both inside and outside of the bedroom among believers and when you add the context of music during sex, it gets intense! We recently witnessed a heated public discussion online about "love making music" among Christian couples. A pastor raised an interesting question about a wife who wanted to play worship music while having sex and her husband who felt that it was a major turn-off. There were over 270 comments on the post and the large majority of people described the wife as someone who was too super spiritual, too heavenly minded, out of order, in need of serious counseling, and even mentally ill. Let's address some of the most common issues raised by those who were appalled by the wife's desire for worship music in the bedroom:

"Intimacy with your spouse is not the time to worship God. You should be ministering only to him or her."

A time of intimacy with your spouse is absolutely a time to worship God together, and in fact that's the premise of this book! It's time for Christian couples to abandon the separation of sexual intimacy from the Creator of sexual intimacy, and allow the fragrance of your worship to be pleasing to Him. Our very lives should be yielded as an offering in worship to the Lover of our Souls. Consider Romans 12:1 which says "Therefore, I urge you, brothers and sisters, in view of God's mercy, to offer your bodies as a living sacrifice, holy and pleasing to God—this is your true and proper worship." Consider whether your soundtrack would be pleasing to Him.

"There's no way you can feel "turned on" by church music!"

There is a rich diversity in music available to explore. We have personally made worship music or no music at all our soundtrack. When you find artists who have deep intimacy with the Lord, the love songs are pure at heart and beautiful. These artists are writing songs to the Lover of their souls and if you were unfamiliar with the artist you could think that the lyrics are referring to a couple in love.

"If you're being intimate with worship music in the bedroom, then when you hear it at church your mind will immediately go into intimacy mode."

Your mind will indeed go into intimacy mode, but it will be intimacy with the Father. When you allow the Lover of your Souls to be involved in your bedroom activities, it is going to transform your intimacy – it will transcend the physical act of the sexual intercourse. You are three parts - spirit, soul (mind, will, emotions), and body (flesh). Whatever you feed is going to take first position, so if your bedroom soundtrack is music that feeds your spirit, then your spirit is going to be in the prominent position whenever you hear it. Your spirit will override what's going on in your mind, with your will and emotions, and with the desires of your flesh.

The next time you hop into the bed, we challenge you to step out in faith, stretch outside of your comfort zone, and try something new with your soundtrack.

Questions To Ask Each Other & Discuss:

1. What's our current soundtrack and what are the implications of it?

2. What are some songs that bring back memories for you?

3. What would you like for our bedroom soundtrack to sound like? Should we make a change?

---

4. What does Romans 12:1 mean to you ("offer your bodies as a living sacrifice")?

Bedroom Lesson #6

Together You're a Prayer

In Ephesians 6:12, the Apostle Paul writes "For our struggle is not against flesh and blood, but against the rulers, against the authorities, against the powers of this dark world and against the spiritual forces of evil in the heavenly realms." The enemy, while invisible to you, seeks to pull husbands and wives apart and destroy your marriage, typically through deception, temptations, and accusations. The good news is that you have power against the enemy and have been equipped with everything you need to be victorious.

Paul refers to the importance of believers putting on the full armor of God, continuously praying in the Holy Spirit to protect from the schemes of the enemy. Prayer is simply communicating with God, and while you may not have ever considered it, you and your spouse having sex as worship unto the Lord can actually serve as a powerfully anointed prayer. There is an anointing of the Holy Spirit that is poured out when a husband and wife join together and unite as one in Christ. What is the anointing? It's God's Spirit and power on you and in you for service in the earth enabling you to be a demonstrator of His presence, love, and power. The scriptures tells us that in partnership with God and His empowerment, one can put 1,000 to flight, but two can put 10,000 to flight (Deuteronomy 32:30). There is great power and strength against evil with your unified covenant as husband and wife.

On the Offense

Christ-centered sex is an offensive attack against the enemy, which is why the Bible urges couples not to abstain from it for an extended period of time (1 Corinthians 7:5). Sexual intimacy is a guard against a wedge that Satan desires to form between you and your spouse that can lead to a marriage full of misery or divorce. It is a guard against the poison of bitterness that leads to temptation. With your unity in both spirit and body, there are prayers that go forth during times of sexual intimacy that will protect from future issues in your marriage such as adultery (actual or mental), habitual self-satisfaction, lust, and pornography.

It's not only sex-related issues that will combated by Christ-centered sex, but other problems that creep into marriages such as living separate independent lives, workaholism, and serious communication struggles. The intimacy creates a knitting of hearts, a safe atmosphere conducive for love-filled discussions on tough topics, and a desire and anticipation to spend more time in each other's company. When it comes to sex and communication, so often relationship experts focus on the benefits of couples communicating about sex. Obviously we agree which is why we include discussion questions with each of these bedroom lessons. However, the inverse is equally true – sexual intimacy provides benefits to communication. In our marriage, we've created a well out of our bedroom (remember bedroom lesson #3?) and tackling otherwise difficult conversations is made easier in that atmosphere. Give it a shot!

On the Defense

In an earlier bedroom lesson we talked about the sexual healing which takes place when the Lord is invited into your intimate affairs. Just as sex can serve as an offensive measure to block and guard against future obstacles, sexual sin, mental and emotional strongholds in your relationship, it can just as powerfully serve as a defensive measure to deal with issues you're already facing.

When you're sowing into the spirit versus the flesh, issues of the heart can be healed including restoration and deliverance from problems created in previous relationships. When you invite Jesus into your bedroom, the supernatural gifts of the Holy Spirit can and will flow freely. Together you're a prayer! There are issues that couples automatically seek marital counselors and sex therapists to deal with without first seeking the Lord. By no means are we saying that counselors and therapists aren't beneficial because God works through people, but be led by Holy Spirit when selecting one and never count out the supernatural power and wisdom of God made available to you.

Years before the Lord invaded our bedroom, we referred to sex as "The Cure All" as an ongoing joke because body aches would disappear (an orgasm beats an aspirin much of the time thanks to the endorphins release) and argumentative spirits would vanish. The joke isn't as much of a joke anymore, and now armed with more wisdom and understanding, we're experiencing even greater benefits because God is just that good (better than we even realize). Prayer changes things, and what's awesome is that no matter how much you've experienced of His goodness, you haven't seen anything yet. Now...let us pray!

Questions To Ask Each Other & Discuss:

1. How has sex been a "cure all" for us?

2. What challenges in our marriage do we need to yield to God?

Bedroom Lesson #7

Two Servant Hearts Guarantee Victory

Serving is at the heart of God. It's His nature. He served by sending His son Jesus Christ, and then served by giving us the Holy Spirit to dwell within us. Jesus told the disciples that the greatest in the Kingdom is the greatest servant; that anyone who desires to be first must be last and servant of all (Mark 9:33-35). This lesson to the disciples applies to marriage as well. Husbands, when you serve your wives, you become her reward. Likewise, wives when you serve your husband, you become his reward. When you make it a competition to be the greatest in your household, everyone wins. You're both competing not to win, but to give each other the advantage.

Looking at Ephesians 5, you'll find wisdom and instruction relevant to operating with a servant's heart within your marriage:

- Walk in love by submitting to one another out of reverence for Christ (verse 21)

- Wives, understand and yield to your husband's leadership as the head of the household (verses 22-24)

- Husbands, love your wife as Christ loved the church; not by domineering, but by cherishing her and giving rather than getting. He gave His life for her (verses 25-26).

Two servant hearts create a Christ-centered culture in your marriage. Jesus said "For even the Son of Man did not come to be served, but to serve, and to give His life a ransom for many." A servant heart results in humility, involvement, and loyalty:

Humility: Humility is not thinking less of yourself, but rather thinking of yourself less. When you're serving your spouse, you have a humble awareness of how you can help and you're mindful of the needs and desires of the one you love. Humility keeps you from setting yourself on the throne, and keeps God on the throne of your heart.

Involvement: As husband and wife you work as a team, but when a decision cannot be jointly agreed upon, the husband is responsible for making that decision. A heart of service creates an environment where the thoughts and feelings of each spouse matters and a loving line of communication remains open on issues related to the marriage and family. A heart of service results in a wife offering encouragement and counsel to the husband, and a husband with an open ear to his wife.

Loyalty: When you put the needs and desires of your spouse ahead of your own, it shows your spouse that he/she is loved and valued which strengthens faithfulness and devotion in the relationship.

Dying Daily

God is always looking at man's heart. Jesus said that we'll be known as His disciples for how we love. Before ascending back to the Father, Jesus asked Peter three times if he loved him, and told him that the way to show that he did is by feeding His sheep, meaning serving His people (John 21:15-19). True love serves and the biggest way you can serve God is by serving others who belong to Him, including your spouse.

If you're going to have a victorious marriage, the way to having a servant's heart is to die to yourself. You have to die daily! You have to make a conscious decision to surrender your life to Christ, being led by the Holy Spirit instead of your flesh. When you make that conscious decision and yield to the Lord, He will help you. You can't make that decision once. You have to make that decision every day. The Holy Spirit will lead you in very practical ways and give you wisdom and insight into what you should do, particularly in instances when there may be challenges in communication with your spouse.

Ministry, Not Manipulation

Two servant hearts will positively impact every area of your marriage, both inside and outside of the bedroom. Unfortunately oftentimes our service to our spouses is actually self-serving. We're giving and serving motivated by what we'll get in return versus being motivated by the love of Christ. When you invite the Lord into your bedroom, maintaining a true servant's heart in your sexual intimacy is not only possible, but it's sweatless.

PHIL: An Addiction Broken and a Change of Heart

I'm always chasing after my wife; that's just what men do who love their wives. However, the reason I'm chasing her has changed. I'm no longer chasing after the orgasm. In fact, I don't even need to have an orgasm all the time anymore. Orgasms are a powerful addiction of our minds, like sugar. Some studies have shown that sugar is eight times more addictive than cocaine! Now that's addictive! While it's true that I was chasing the orgasm, I wasn't all about "getting mine." I was focused on ensuring that my wife got hers first, but it was still selfishly motivated because I was giving primarily to gain recognition and maintain reputation.

Once we yielded ourselves to the Lord in the bedroom, things changed. I no longer focus on myself. I desire to give my wife the advantage. Of course I still enjoy having orgasms, but the addiction is broken. I still enjoy ensuring my wife has one first, but it's motivated by a pure heart to give to her rather than selfishness. I know that I will receive as a result of my giving (and I do receive!), but I'm giving because the Lord has helped me become more like Him. I'm still chasing after my wife, but it's because I'm excited to give to her and shower her with my love… and shower the Lord with my love as well. I'm most interested in what the time of intimacy does for us collectively.

Serve in Love

Partner with God in serving your spouse, because when you partner with God, you'll have the right heart and loving attitude about your service. Give thought and attention to what your husband or wife would appreciate in your sexual intimacy. Your husband loves a specific football team? Grab a cute jersey with his favorite team and wear it to bed before or after the game! Your wife prefers bikini briefs over your comfy and trusty boxer briefs? Buy a few pair and switch out of your boxers before you get ready to play with your wife. Your husband loves the smell of one of your perfumes? Take a shower and splash a little on before you get into bed. Your wife is feeling stressed with the housework and cleaning? Don't just tell her that the sex will de-stress her. Help her out (it's awesome foreplay)!

Remember that when it comes to marriage, what takes place inside of the bedroom impacts what happens outside of the bedroom. Likewise what happens outside of the bedroom impacts what happens inside of the bedroom. Choose each day to give your spouse the advantage, both inside and outside of the bedroom, and victory is absolutely guaranteed.

Questions To Ask Each Other & Discuss:

1. What can I do to be of more help to you?

2. How can I better serve you in our sexual intimacy?

Bedroom Lesson #8

Your Appetite Will Change

The final bedroom lesson is simply that your appetite will change once you've invited the Lord into your sexual intimacy. It's similar to your natural appetite with food. As you experience different foods, flavor combinations, and higher quality foods your palate becomes more discriminating. Have you ever experienced trying a food as an adult that you loved as a child and now find it to be inedible or unsatisfying? Have you ever changed your diet for an extended period of time and then found that you were unable to return to some of the things you used to eat? We had this experience in our family with maple syrup. Our entire lives we only experienced the popular syrups on the grocery shelves with the main ingredient being high fructose corn syrup; we'd never had pure maple syrup. Once we experienced pure maple syrup and used it for several months, we were no longer able to enjoy our old family favorite, Mrs. Butterworth's. When we attempted to use it on our pancakes again, everyone in the family (including our 6 year old daughter) immediately noticed the difference and no longer enjoyed it; some of our stomachs just rejected it completely. Our appetites had changed.

The scripture tells us in Psalm 107 that He "satisfies the thirsty and fills the hungry with good things." Satisfying the flesh during sex feels really good, and there is nothing wrong or displeasing to the Lord for you to do so if it's done in a way that honors your spouse. However, if you want to be filled with good things from the Lord through your sexual intimacy that will overflow into every single part of your marriage in supernatural ways, then you have to be hungry. God rewards those who diligently seek Him (Hebrews 11:6), and His rewards are GREAT. As you taste more of God in your bedroom, you'll crave more of Him and your appetite will change.

You may be thinking about some of the exciting things that you're doing in your bedroom now and wondering whether you actually want your appetite to change. You may be thinking "Phil and Shae, you just don't understand! The way my wife/husband works it in the bedroom, I'm already screaming 'Hallelujah!' It's fun and a little bit freaky and we do plenty of thanking God for it!" We actually do understand, and a couple years ago we would have said the same thing. There are things we used to thoroughly enjoy doing in bedroom; things we could not imagine giving up voluntarily. The truth is that we actually never gave them up, we simply experienced something greater and our appetite changed. A series of encounters with Him in our bedroom increased our hunger and led to a greater pursuit to know more of Him. Like the loving Father He is, He responded.

Whatever you yield to the Lord and place at the feet of Jesus, He offers you an amazing exchange. You always get the better end of the deal. Always! Don't take our word for it. Taste and see for yourself that the Lord (even in your bedroom) is good!

Questions To Ask Each Other & Discuss:

1. Have you ever experienced an appetite change? How did you feel about that change? Did you feel like you were missing out?

2. How do you feel about the fact that our appetite may change in the bedroom?

The Pursuit

Despite its challenges, marriage is a joyous and precious privilege. A Christ-centered marriage is not defined as two people who are married and just happen to be Christian. A Christ-centered marriage is a transformative one with continual growth that serves as a reflection of the union of Christ and His Church. A Christ-centered marriage is one where two people who have made Jesus Christ the Lord of their lives humbly pour themselves into the life of their spouse, loving unconditionally and serving each other empowered daily by the grace of an Almighty God and the power of the Holy Spirit.

Perhaps you're reading this book alone and your spouse refused to read it because he or she has not made Jesus Christ Lord. If that's you, be encouraged. God is not taken by surprise by your situation. He already knows your end from the beginning. As you behold (set your eyes upon) Christ, your marriage goes from one level of glory to another. Provide the Lord with access to your relationship and He will bring about the change. Take the lessons you've learned in this book, implement what you're able to do, and watch the faithfulness of God in action.

If you're reading this and you haven't given your life to the Lord, or perhaps you have asked Jesus into your heart, but you haven't made Him Lord of your life, we invite you to say this prayer:

"Father, thank you for loving me unconditionally. I need you in my life. I ask You to forgive me of all of my sins. By faith, I believe that your son Jesus Christ died for me, was resurrected from the dead, is alive, and hears my prayer. I invite Jesus to become the Lord of my life, to rule and reign in my heart from this day forward. Fill me with Your Holy Spirit so that I may live victoriously in Jesus, with strength, wisdom, and determination to walk in the center of Your will for the rest of my life. In Jesus' name, I pray, Amen."

Congratulations, and get ready for an awesome adventure with God!

Our objective with this book is to ignite marriages worldwide by igniting bedrooms with the power and love of God. We pray that you have been blessed and empowered by these bedroom lessons and by the resulting discussions you've had as a couple. At a minimum, you should have plenty of food for thought and something to seek God about for yourself. At best, you will experience more than you ever imagined in your marriage as you pursue more of God through your sexual intimacy.

The Lord wants to be involved in your bedroom. He desires to be involved in every area of your life because He loves you; so much so that He sacrificed His only Son for you and then gave you the Holy Spirit to dwell inside of you and help you live life more abundantly. He truly is the Lover of your soul.

Pursue Him with your entire heart, trust Him and include Him in every aspect of your marriage (inside and outside the bedroom), knowing that He will respond with a greater portion of Himself. We promise that your marriage will never be the same.

Ask Phil and Shae

(What You May Be Thinking)

Writing a book on a topic like having a ménage à trois between you, your spouse, and the Lover of your souls is bound to create a lot of reactions and plenty of questions, so we want to address many of those upfront.

About the Book (General)

Why a ménage à trois? Sounds pretty freaky for a book for Christians!

Shae: Great question. I actually wondered the same thing when the Holy Spirit gave that phrase to me for the book. When I heard Him say it, I didn't even really know what the word meant. I knew what it meant in our American culture, but I didn't know what the origins of the word were or what it actually meant in French. The phrase ménage à trois is French for "household of three." It's actually the perfect word to use to describe the idea of inviting the Lord into our bedroom affairs. It got your attention, right? I'm certain that was all by His design. God is intentional.

Did you seriously get all 8 of these lessons while you were having sex?

Phil: Either during or immediately afterwards!

Shae: It was pretty crazy. Sometimes we'd just get the name of a chapter and had to ask later what it meant. Other times we'd receive the entire lesson.

This whole book sounded crazy to me. Am I supposed to take this seriously?

Phil: Think this is crazy? No problem at all. I suggest just praying in your bed together as a couple. This will begin to create a well in your bedroom. The more of God that is in a room, the more of Him you will get in that room.

Shae: That's up to you! The things of God are spiritually discerned, so if this all sounds crazy I encourage you to pray, ask the Lord to open your eyes to the things you need to see and open your heart to receive...then read it again!

Inviting the Lord in the Bedroom

My husband/wife and I really love our freaky positions! Are you saying that we should stop them?

Phil: I can't tell you that answer. Remember there is freedom in your marriage bed as long as you're honoring your spouse. I can ask you this though....Is God pleased with your freaky positions? Just the fact that you're calling them freaky could be an issue. God's concern is our hearts and acting out of faith, not sin. If you have faith that God is pleased, go for it. If you don't, why would you do it if your objective is to glorify Him?

Shae: Once you've invited the Lord into your bedroom affairs, He is going to speak. If the Holy Spirit convicts you about something you're doing in the bed, don't do it. If one of you is uncomfortable for some reason with a particular position, don't do it. If you believe you're honoring God and honoring each other, go for it but just don't put God in a box. Go for greater. Go for more. Seek Him for something that you just may find to be even more awesome than what you're enjoying now.

This all sounds so "super spiritual." Do you guys have any fun in the bedroom anymore?

Shae: Yes! Inviting Jesus in the bedroom makes things anything but dull. I'll spare you the details, but we encourage you to give the things we shared in this book a shot and discover the adventure for yourselves. In fact, LIFE with Jesus is fun. The more acquainted with the Lord I get, the more I understand the scripture that says that God uses the foolish things to confound the wise. Following God is a wild and crazy and an absolutely amazing adventure. He's never boring.

Bedroom Conflicts

Ok, I'm sold on this idea of inviting the Lord into our bedroom but my husband/wife is not interested in this. Now what?

Phil: Rest assured that if there's just one person who is inviting the Lord into the bedroom, then He is invited. When it comes to you, your spouse, and the Lover of your souls, you and the Lord are already the majority. You opening the door is all the access He needs and He'll elevate you as you are going after Him, all while working on the heart of your spouse. Keep in mind that "heart work" starts internally and then manifests externally, so it may take a little time for you to see the visible evidence.

Keep honoring your spouse and focus your heart and attention on God, even if your spouse hasn't given his/her heart to Jesus yet. He knows your heart. You don't even have to make any verbal announcements that you've invited Him in because when you focus on Him, you draw Him near to you and your spouse will benefit from His presence as well.

I've been hurt in previous relationships which makes it hard for me to believe that this is possible with my husband. What should I do?

Shae: The first step is forgiving the person or people who hurt you in previous relationships. You have to allow the Lord to heal you from that hurt and forgiveness is where that starts. Once you've done that, you're in a better position emotionally and spiritually to open yourself up to inviting the Lord in your bedroom and experiencing the greater with your husband. You can do it!

Shae, seriously are you always in the mood for this? I'm often not in the mood to have sex.

Shae: No, but I've found that when I choose to serve and just take steps to prepare myself for intimate time, the feeling of "I'm not in the mood" often goes away. Also, I can tell you that ever since we invited the Lord in our bedroom, the time it takes to go from "I'm not in the mood" to "I'm ready" has shortened dramatically. Just another one of the perks!

Ménage à Trois Discussion Questions

Lesson #1: The Lord Wants to Be Involved in Your Bedroom

1. How do you feel about inviting Jesus in our bedroom?

2. What does worship mean to you? Can you see how sex can be offered as worship?

3. What are 3 things that you appreciate most about me?

Lesson #2: Intimacy with Each Other Begins with Intimacy with God

1. Do you feel like you have an intimate relationship with God?

2. How do you talk to God and how does He speak to you?

3. Have you ever experienced Holy Spirit giving you an instruction that helped you in our marriage? Tell me about it.

Lesson #3: Your Bedroom Is a Well

1. Have you personally dug a well anywhere inside or outside of our home? Tell me about an experience or encounter you had with the Lord there.

2. What would Heaven on earth in our marriage look like to you?

Lesson #4: Sow Into the Spirit, Not the Flesh

1. How can I best honor you in our sexual intimacy?

2. Is there anything that we do in the bedroom that makes you uncomfortable?

3. Are we making a climax an idol? How so? What can we do to change that? Do you want to change that?

4. Have you ever felt convicted by the Holy Spirit regarding something we've done in the bedroom?

5. What does "sowing to the spirit" look like to you? How can we begin to do that more in our physical intimacy?

Lesson #5: What's Your Soundtrack?

1. What's our current soundtrack and what are the implications of it?

2. What are some songs that bring back memories for you?

3. What would you like for our bedroom soundtrack to sound like? Should we make a change?

4. What does Romans 12:1 mean to you ("offer your bodies as a living sacrifice")?

Lesson #6: Together You're a Prayer

1. How has sex been a "cure all" for us?

2. What challenges in our marriage do we need to yield to God?

Lesson #7: Two Servant Hearts Guarantee a Victory

1. What can I do to be of more help to you?

2. How can I better serve you in our sexual intimacy?

Lesson #8: Your Appetite Will Change

1. Have you ever experienced an appetite change? How did you feel about that change? Did you feel like you were missing out?

2. How do you feel about the fact that our appetite may change in the bedroom?

Ménage à Trois 14-Day Couples Bible Study

Making a habit of reading Bible together as a couple is a powerful way to strengthen your union. Below are scriptures referenced in this book that we recommend meditating on and discussing together.

You may want to have one spouse read aloud to the other and consider reading these passages of scripture in multiple translations.

Day 1:   Living as Those Made Alive in Christ
             Colossians 3:1-17

Day 2:   Instructions for Christian Households
             Colossians 3:18-25

Day 3:   A Psalm for Giving Grateful Praise
             Psalm 100

Day 4:   Life Through the Spirit
             Romans 8:1-16

Day 5:   More Than Conquerors
             Romans 8:31-39

Day 6:   A Prayer and Praise for Protection
             Psalm 91

Day 7:   The Greater Glory of the New Covenant
          2 Corinthians 3:1-18

Day 8:   John Teaches Nicodemus
          John 3:1-17

Day 9:   Freedom in Christ
          Galatians 5:1-26

Day 10:   Exhortation for Couples
          Hebrews 13:1-8

Day 11:   A Living Sacrifice
          Romans 12:1-21

Day 12:   Married Life
          1 Corinthians 7:1-15

Day 13:   Instructions for Christian Households
          Ephesians 5:21-33

Day 14:   A Praise for God's Goodness
          Psalm 107

About The Authors

Phil and Shae Bynes are a couple of crazy kids in love who have been married for 25 years and together as best friends since high school. They are committed to helping the body of Christ experience God's best and have greater Kingdom impact through their personal and professional lives.

Phil is CEO of KingdomDrivenEntrepreneur.com, which serves entrepreneurs who desire to do business in partnership with God, led and empowered by Holy Spirit. He is also a licensed massage therapist of over 20 years and the owner of Crazy Good Massage.

Affectionately known as 'Chief Fire Igniter,' Shae is a pioneer in the Kingdom entrepreneurship movement who has touched the hearts and minds of over one million people through her writing, speaking, and mentoring since 2012. She is a corporate transformation consultant and the Founder and Executive Advisor for Kingdom Driven LLC.

Phil and Shae reside in the Fort Lauderdale, Florida area and have three beautiful daughters, Anisa, Nia, and Malia.

Connect With The Authors

Connect with Phil:

E-mail: info@kingdomdrivenentrepreneur.com

LinkedIn: linkedin.com/in/philbynes/

Connect with Shae:

E-mail: info@shaebynes.com

LinkedIn: linkedin.com/in/shaebynes

www.ingramcontent.com/pod-product-compliance
Lightning Source LLC
Chambersburg PA
CBHW060137050426
42448CB00010B/2170